SKIING

A TRUE BOOK

by

Larry Dane Brimner

Children's Press®
A Division of Grolier Publishing

New York London Hong Kong Sydney
Danbury, Connecticut

U.S. skier
Tommy Moe

Reading Consultant
Linda Cornwell
Learning Resource Consultant
Indiana Department
of Education

Author's Dedication:
For Brendan January

Library of Congress Cataloging-in-Publication Data

Brimner, Larry Dane.
   Skiing / by Larry Dane Brimner.
      p.   cm.—(A true book)
   Includes bibliographical references (p.).
   Summary: Illustrates the various styles of skiing, from cross-country to
downhill, as well as kinds of equipment and clothing.
   ISBN 0-516-20449-1 (lib. bdg.)   0-516-26205-X (pbk.)
   1. Skis and skiing. [1. Skis and skiing.] I. Title. II. Series.
GV854.B687 1997
796.93—dc21
                                                  97-12829
                                                   CIP
                                                     AC

Contents

Eddie Edwards' cheerful sense of humor made him a celebrity at the 1988 Winter Olympics in Calgary, Canada.

The Eagle Flies

At the 1988 Olympics in Calgary, Canada, Eddie Edwards became known to the world as "Eddie the Eagle." At the age of 24, he was the most popular ski jumper in Olympic history. No one captured the world's sense of Olympic humor the way Eddie did.

He had no money. He had very little training. But Eddie

had enthusiasm. He also held Great Britain's record in ski jumping. Of course, he was Great Britain's only ski jumper! Other ski jumpers sailed gracefully through the air when they jumped. Eddie's jumps were like a baby bird's first flight. He flapped his arms and twisted his body to keep his balance. Still, people admired his spunk.

Eddie borrowed his equipment—skis from the Austrians, a helmet from the Italians, and

Eddie struggles to keep his balance during a jump (left). Although he finished last in both jumping events, Eddie could still take pride in his achievements (right).

a ski suit from the Germans. When the final scores were tallied, he finished in last place. But Eddie didn't mind. He had tried—and that, after all, is the spirit of the Olympics.

The Events

Skiing has been part of the Olympic Winter Games since they were first held in 1924. Over the years, different skiing events have been added to the Winter Olympics. They offer a wide variety of excitement and drama.

Skiing is divided into two main types—Alpine and

Alpine skiers need speed to win races.

Nordic. The word "Alpine" refers to the European mountains called the Alps. Alpine skiing events take place on mountain slopes. These events test a skier's strength, control, and ability to ski with speed. They include the downhill, the slalom, the giant slalom, and the super G.

The word "Nordic" refers to Scandinavian and other snowy regions in northern Europe. Many skiing events come from these lands. The Nordic events fall into two very different categories—ski jumping and cross-country racing. The only thing they have in common is long distance. Ski

Ski jumpers (above) compete for style and distance. Cross-country skiing (left) demands endurance.

jumpers strive for the longest jump. Cross-country skiers race against the clock over long courses.

Alpine Skiing

In the **downhill event**, each skier bursts from the starting gate and follows a course down a mountain slope to the finish line. The skiers speed down straightaways, around sharp bends, and over sudden drop-offs. Downhill racers can approach speeds of eighty

A downhill skier jumps out of the starting gate (left). Speeding down the slope, the skier (below) tries to beat the other racers' times to win.

miles per hour. At such high speeds, one wrong move can bring a skier crashing down.

In the Olympics, downhill races are decided by a single run. The skier with the fastest time wins.

The downhill skiing event has been part of the Olympics since 1948. Most of the medals have been won by French, Swiss, Austrian, and German skiers. At the 1994 Lillehammer Games in Norway, however, Tommy Moe took home a gold medal and Picabo Street won a silver

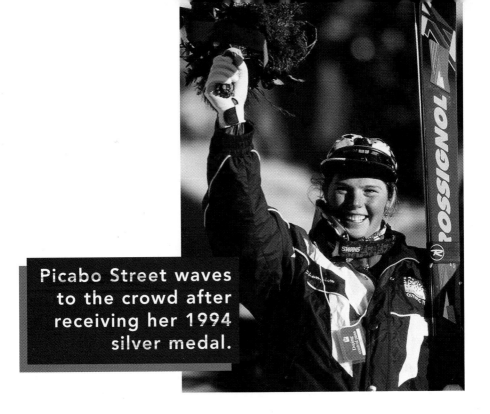

Picabo Street waves to the crowd after receiving her 1994 silver medal.

medal in the women's division. Both skied for the United States.

The **slalom race** tests a skier's control. The race course is a series of turns marked by red and blue flags called "gates."

In the slalom (left), racers must ski around a series of gates. Switzerland's Vreni Schneider (above) skies around a gate during a slalom race. She wears guards to protect her shins and knees from the poles.

The gate is a flexible pole planted firmly in the snow. Slalom skiers turn so tightly around each gate that they knock the poles over. The poles are designed to spring back upright. The skiers wear special guards to protect their legs and arms.

A slalom skier must cut around each gate without missing any of them. Only a short distance separates each gate. In Olympic competition, winning skiers make a turn about every second or less. The men's course has 55 to 75 gates; the women's course has 45 to 60.

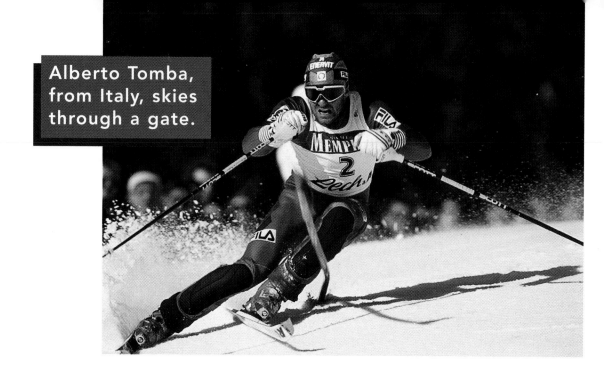

Alberto Tomba, from Italy, skies through a gate.

Competitors make two runs, and the medal goes to the skier with the fastest combined time. Recent Olympic champions in the slalom have been Phil Mahre of the United States (1984), Alberto Tomba of Italy (1988), and Petra Kronberger of Austria (1992).

A **giant slalom** course is longer than a slalom course. The distance between each gate is greater, so the racers can ski faster. They must cut

Gates in the giant slalom are larger than those used in the slalom.

around 35 to 45 gates on the men's course and 30 to 40 gates on the women's. In recent years, this event has been dominated by skiers from Italy, Switzerland, and Austria.

The **super giant slalom** event, or super G, joined Olympic competition in 1988. It is called the super G because skiers must make sharp turns at extremely high speeds. Like the giant slalom, this event tests both speed

Skiers must have great control to maneuver through the super giant slalom course.

and control. The course is longer than the giant slalom course but shorter than the downhill course. The distance between each gate is also greater than in the giant slalom, enabling skiers to speed up to 60 miles per hour.

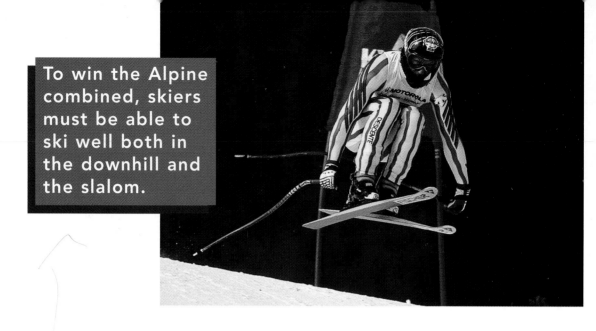

To win the Alpine combined, skiers must be able to ski well both in the downhill and the slalom.

The **Alpine combined** event was held from 1936 to 1948 before it was discontinued for forty years. It returned to the Olympic lineup in 1988. On the first day of competition, skiers race the downhill course. The next day, they complete two slalom runs over different courses. The winner is decided by combining the three scores.

Nordic Skiing

The idea behind **ski jumping** is simple. A skier swoops down a snowy ramp, launches into the air, and flies as far as possible before touching down again on the snow. Jumps are scored by distance jumped and by style. Jumpers compete on the "normal hill" or "large hill." Normal hill jumps are about 90 meters

This view of a ski jump course (above) shows the "normal hill" ski jump on the left, and the "large hill" ski jump on the right. Ski jumpers (right) take three jumps during Olympic competition.

(295 feet) in distance. Large hill jumps stretch out about 120 meters (394 feet). Only men compete in Olympic ski-jumping events.

Competitors make three jumps. The first one is for practice, but the next two count. The distances reached on the last two jumps are added together. This score is combined with points earned for style. The jumper with the highest total score wins the competition.

At the top of a ski jump, a skier goes when the light turns green.

Ski jumping got its start in Norway and was an event at the very first Olympic Winter Games. In the early years, Norway won most of the Olympic medals for ski jumping. Today, Finland, Austria, and Germany dominate the sport.

Cross-country skiing includes several races. They differ only in the distance raced and the skiing style used. There are two styles of cross-country skiing—classic and freestyle. In the classic style, a skier keeps both skis parallel. Pushing with long poles, he or she moves for-ward in gliding strides. In freestyle, a skier uses a skating motion that is faster than the classic style. Freestyle cross-

In freestyle cross-country skiing (left), the skiers use a skating motion to move faster. In classic style cross-country skiing (right), the skiers must keep their skis parallel.

country skiing wasn't allowed in the Olympics until 1988.

Many experts say that cross-country skiing is the most physically demanding of all the Winter Olympic sports. Cross-country races are up to 50 kilometers for men and 30 kilometers for women. Only the fittest athletes can compete and win.

The **biathlon** began as a military exercise in 1767. It combines Nordic skiing and rifle-shooting—skills that were, and still are, important to soldiers patrolling snow-covered lands. The biathlon became part of the Olympics in 1960. The event requires

In the biathlon, cross-country skiers pause to shoot targets.

each skier to follow a set course. Along the way, he or she must stop to shoot at targets—sometimes from a standing position and sometimes while lying down.

The **Nordic combined** is a two-day event. Skiers jump the normal ski-jumping hill on the first day and race a 15-kilometer cross-country course on the second day. Some say that the winner of the Nordic combined is the *meister*, or master, of Nordic sports.

Some people claim that the winner of the Nordic combined is the master of Nordic sports.

Summer Fun

When the days grow long and temperatures rise, most skiers pack up their equipment and wait for next winter. But Winter Olympic athletes don't head for the beach. For them, summer is just another training season. Ski jumpers slide down ramps covered with slippery mats. Downhill skiers attach rollers to their skis and race down grass-covered slopes. Acrobatic skiers launch themselves into the air before landing safely in a pool!

Faster and Higher

To get as much speed as possible, skiers use some special tricks to reduce air resistance. When a skier is racing down a slope, the skier's body impacts the air. The air is like a thick wall that slows the skier. The bigger the skier's body, the harder it is to cut

Alpine skiers crouch low to cut through the air easily (left). This skier (right) crouches before going down a steep slope.

through this wall of air. To increase their speed, skiers try to make themselves as small as possible. They ski in a tucked position and use poles that curve behind them. As much as possible, they try to resemble a speeding bullet.

Ski jumpers arch their backs to catch more air and increase the length of their jumps.

How do ski jumpers fly higher? When they launch themselves off the ramp, they stretch forward. This helps them slice through the air. They also arch their backs so that their bodies act like the wings of an airplane. Just as an airplane's wings help lift it into the air, ski jumpers are lifted by arching their backs.

The Newcomers

Freestyle skiing developed in the 1960s. Young skiers, tired of traditional skiing, wanted to do something different. They began performing acrobatic stunts and aerial (in the air) maneuvers. Some even tried ski ballet. As a result, two new sports were added to the Olympic medal events:

Ski ballet artists twist and turn on their skis.

moguls (in 1992) and aerials (in 1994).

In **moguls skiing**, a skier encounters about seventy-five moguls, or small hills. The skier must ski quickly, because this is a race against the clock.

Mogul skiers maneuver down slopes covered with small hills (left). While twisting among the moguls, skiers must also perform stunts (right).

At the same time, though, the skier must perform acrobatic stunts with names like the "twister," the "daffy," and the "spread-eagle." Somersaults are not permitted.

An aerial skier launches off a ramp (left). In the air, the aerial skier performs difficult twists and somersaults (right).

Aerial skiing requires real showmanship. In this event, the skier launches from a ramp and performs acrobatics as high as three stories above the ground.

In aerial skiing, each skier must perform somersaults. Single, double, and even triple somersaults are all used to impress the judges.

Another newcomer to the Olympics is **snowboarding**. It will be a medal event at the 1998 Winter Games in Nagano, Japan. Like freestyle skiing, snowboarding started in the 1960s when young people began to look for a new challenge on the slopes. For many,

Snowboarding will become a medal sport in the 1998 Winter Olympics. Snowboarders perform special stunts in the half pipe (right).

snowboards were the answer. In snowboarding, both of the skiers' feet are attached to what looks like a fat, single ski. Men and women will compete separately in giant slalom and half pipe events. The half pipe events take place in a U-shaped trench in the snow. Like aerial skiing, half-pipe snowboarding includes airborne stunts and acrobatics.

Olympic athletes are always striving to be better. So, too, are the Olympic Games. Olympic sports have changed with the times so that new generations of athletes will have an arena in which to perform—an arena in which to try.

To Find Out More

Here are some additional resources to help you learn more about skiing:

 **Books**

Bailey, Donna. **Skiing.** Sports World, 1990.

Bartges, Dan. **Winter Games Made Simple: A Guide for Spectators & Television Viewers.** Turner Publishing, Inc., 1993.

Brimner, Larry Dane. **The Winter Olympics.** Children's Press, 1997.

Greenspan, Bud. **100 Greatest Moments in Olympic History.** General Publishing Group, 1995.

Haycock, Kate. **Skiing.** Crestwood House, 1991.

Malley, Stephen. **A Kid's Guide to the Nineteen Ninety-Four Winter Olympics.** Bantam Press, 1994.

Organizations and Online Sites

2002 Winter Olympic Games Home Page
http://www.SLC2002.org

A growing web page that provides information on the 2002 Winter Olympics in Salt Lake City.

Cross Country & Nordic Skiing Information Center
http://www.xcski.org/

An extensive site that lists areas to ski, conditions, and necessary equipment.

Official 1998 Olympic Web Site
http://www.nagano.olympic.org

A great source of information on the events of the 1998 Winter Olympics.

An Olympic Games Primer
http://www.aafla.com/pubs/olyprim.htm

An exciting site that introduces the Olympic games.

U.S. Biathlon Association (USBA)
421 Old Military Road
Lake Placid, NY 12946

U.S. Ski Team
http://www.usskiteam.com/

A great site that provides schedules and information about the U.S. Ski Team and several links to other skiing-related sites.

U.S. Skiing (USSA)
P.O. Box 100
Park City, UT 84060

Winter Sports Page
http://www.wintersports.org

A central site to explore winter sports and links to other sites.

Important Words

air resistance force that slows down an object as it moves through air

alpine combined event that has three races: the downhill and the long and short slalom

Alpine skiing downhill skiing

gates flags that indicate turns to slalom skiers

moguls bumps or small hills made of snow

Nordic skiing cross-country skiing and ski jumping

slalom event in which a skier must ski around gates

super giant slalom event that combines slalom and downhill, also called the "super G"

Index

Meet the Author

Larry Dane Brimner is the author of several books for Children's Press, including five True Books on the Winter Olympics. He is a member of the Authors Guild and the Society of Children's Book Writers and Illustrators. Mr. Brimner makes his home in Southern California and the Rocky Mountains.